MARCHA CRIANÇA

1º ANO ENSINO FUNDAMENTAL

LÍNGUA INGLESA

Eliete Canesi Morino
Graduada pela Pontifícia Universidade Católica de São Paulo (PUC-SP) em Língua e Literatura Inglesa e Tradução e Interpretação.
Especialização em Língua Inglesa pela International Bell School of London.
Pós-graduada em Metodologia da Língua Inglesa pela Faculdade de Tecnologia e Ciência.
Atuou como professora na rede particular de ensino e em projetos comunitários.

Rita Brugin de Faria
Graduada pela Faculdade de Arte Santa Marcelina e pela Faculdade Paulista de Arte.
Especialização em Língua Inglesa pela International Bell School of London.
Pós-graduada em Metodologia da Língua Inglesa pela Faculdade de Tecnologia e Ciência.
Especialista em alfabetização, atuou como professora e coordenadora pedagógica nas redes pública e particular de ensino.

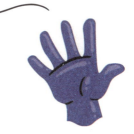

editora scipione

editora scipione

Presidência: Mario Ghio Júnior
Direção editorial: Lidiane Vivaldini Olo
Gerência editorial: Viviane Carpegiani
Gestão de área: Tatiany Renó (Anos Iniciais)
Edição: Mariangela Secco (coord.), Ana Lucia Militello, Carla Fernanda Nascimento, Maiza Prande Bernardello
Planejamento e controle de produção: Flávio Matuguma, Juliana Batista, Felipe Nogueira e Juliana Gonçalves
Revisão: Hélia de Jesus Gonsaga (ger.), Kátia Scaff Marques (coord.), Rosângela Muricy (coord.), Ana Paula C. Malfa, Brenda T. M. Morais, Carlos Eduardo Sigrist, Daniela Lima, Diego Carbone, Flavia S. Vênezio, Gabriela M. Andrade, Heloísa Schiavo, Hires Heglan, Kátia S. Lopes Godoi, Luciana B. Azevedo, Luís M. Boa Nova, Luiz Gustavo Bazana, Malvina Tomáz, Patricia Cordeiro, Patrícia Travanca, Paula T. de Jesus, Ricardo Miyake, Sandra Fernandez, Sueli Bossi e Vanessa P. Santos; Bárbara de M. Genereze (estagiária)
Arte: Claudio Faustino (ger.), Erika Tiemi Yamauchi (coord.), Keila Cristina Grandis (edição de arte)
Diagramação: Ponto Inicial Design Gráfico
Iconografia e tratamento de imagem: Sílvio Kligin (ger.), Claudia Bertolazzi (coord.), Camila Losimfeldt (pesquisa), Fernanda Crevin (tratamento de imagens)
Licenciamento de conteúdos de terceiros: Roberta Bento (gerente); Jenis Oh (coord.); Liliane Rodrigues e Flávia Zambon (analistas); Raísa Maris Reina (assist.)
Ilustrações: Paula Kranz (Aberturas de unidade), Ari Nicolosi, Ilustra Cartoon, Marimbando e Sirayama
Design: Gláucia Correa Koller (ger.), Flávia Dutra e Gustavo Vanini (proj. gráfico e capa), Erik Taketa (pós-produção)
Ilustração de capa: Estúdio Luminos

Todos os direitos reservados por Somos Sistemas de Ensino S.A.
Avenida Paulista, 901, 6º andar – Bela Vista
São Paulo – SP – CEP 01310-200
http://www.somoseducacao.com.br

Dados Internacionais de Catalogação na Publicação (CIP)

```
Morino, Eliete Canesi
   Marcha Criança : Língua Inglesa : 1º ao 5º ano /
Eliete Canesi Morino, Rita Brugin. -- 3. ed. -- São
Paulo : Scipione, 2020.
   (Coleção Marcha Criança ; vol. 1 ao 5)

   Bibliografia

   1. Língua inglesa (Ensino fundamental) - Anos iniciais
I. Título II. Brugin, Rita III. Série

                                         CDD 372.652
20-1102
```
Angélica Ilacqua - Bibliotecária - CRB-8/7057

2023
Código da obra CL 745884
CAE 721139 (AL) / 721140 (PR)
ISBN 978 85 474 030 34 (AL)
ISBN 978 85 474 030 41 (PR)
3ª edição
5ª impressão
De acordo com a BNCC.

Impressão e acabamento: Bercrom Gráfica e Editora

Com ilustrações de **Paula Kranz**, seguem abaixo os créditos das fotos utilizadas nas aberturas de Unidade:

UNIDADE 1: Telha: Sven Boettcher/Shutterstock, **Árvore:** amornchaijj/Shutterstock, **Casa:** LesPalenik/Shutterstock, **Janela:** vipman/Shutterstock, **Casa amarela:** Ratthaphong Ekariyasap/Shutterstock, **Bola:** irin-k/Shutterstock.

UNIDADE 2: Arbusto oval: BK foto/Shutterstock, **Janela preta:** New Africa/Shutterstock, **Arbusto com flores:** Flower Studio/Shutterstock, **Bicicleta:** sspopov/Shutterstock, **Carro:** awpixel.com/Shutterstock, **Arbusto longo:** BK foto/Shutterstock, **Árvore:** kpboonjit/Shutterstock, **Cadeira de rodas:** Talaj/Shutterstock, **Portas de madeira:** Vaclav Volrab/Shutterstock.

UNIDADE 3: DNA: LuckyStep/Shutterstock, **Textura de cimento:** Rawpixel.com/Shutterstock, **Textura de tintas coloridas:** Sweet Art/Shutterstock, **Monitor:** Den Rozhnovsky/Shutterstock, **Giz de cera:** Lucie Lang/Shutterstock, **Passarinho:** Lucie Lang/Shutterstock.

UNIDADE 4: Gramado: EFKS/Shutterstock, **Coreto:** Noel V. Baebler/Shutterstock, **Motocicleta:** Bonma Suriya/Shutterstock, **Balanço:** photka/Shutterstock, **Árvores:** WARUT PINAMKA/Shutterstock, **Carro vermelho:** Rawpixel.com/Shutterstock, **Ônibus escolar:** docent/Shutterstock, **Escorregador:** LightSecond/Shutterstock, **Janela:** Nerthuz/Shutterstock, **Semáforo:** BOYDTRIPHOTO/Shutterstock, **Arbustos:** Tomas Klema/Shutterstock.

APRESENTAÇÃO

QUERIDO ALUNO, QUERIDA ALUNA,

QUANTO MAIS CEDO COMEÇAMOS A ESTUDAR UMA SEGUNDA LÍNGUA, MAIS SIMPLES E FÁCIL É APRENDÊ-LA.

COM A COLEÇÃO **MARCHA CRIANÇA LÍNGUA INGLESA**, VOCÊ DESCOBRIRÁ QUE A LÍNGUA INGLESA JÁ FAZ PARTE DO DIA A DIA, E ESPERAMOS QUE VOCÊ TENHA PRAZER EM APRENDER ESSE IDIOMA, TÃO NECESSÁRIO PARA ENTENDER MELHOR O MUNDO EM QUE VIVEMOS.

AQUI VOCÊ ENCONTRA UM MODO DIVERTIDO DE APRENDER POR MEIO DE DIVERSAS ATIVIDADES, COMO COLAGENS, DESENHOS, PINTURAS, DRAMATIZAÇÕES, JOGOS, CANÇÕES E MUITO MAIS!

PARTICIPE COM ENTUSIASMO DAS AULAS E APROVEITE ESTA OPORTUNIDADE QUE SEU PROFESSOR E ESTA COLEÇÃO PROPICIAM: APRENDER INGLÊS DE MANEIRA BASTANTE INSTIGANTE E MOTIVADORA.

GOOD JOB!

AS AUTORAS

Paula Kranz/Arquivo da editora

KNOW YOUR BOOK

VEJA A SEGUIR COMO SEU LIVRO ESTÁ ORGANIZADO.

UNIT

SEU LIVRO ESTÁ ORGANIZADO EM QUATRO UNIDADES TEMÁTICAS, COM ABERTURAS EM PÁGINAS DUPLAS. CADA UNIDADE TEM DUAS LIÇÕES. AS ABERTURAS DE UNIDADE SÃO COMPOSTAS DOS SEGUINTES BOXES:

JOIN THE CIRCLE!

VOCÊ E OS COLEGAS TERÃO A OPORTUNIDADE DE CONVERSAR SOBRE A CENA APRESENTADA E A RESPEITO DO QUE JÁ SABEM SOBRE O TEMA DA UNIDADE.

LET'S LEARN!

AQUI VOCÊ VAI ENCONTRAR A LISTA DOS CONTEÚDOS QUE SERÃO ESTUDADOS NA UNIDADE.

LISTEN AND SAY

ESTA SEÇÃO TEM O PROPÓSITO DE FAZER VOCÊ OBSERVAR E EXPLORAR A CENA DE ABERTURA DA LIÇÃO. PERMITE TAMBÉM QUE VOCÊ ENTRE EM CONTATO COM AS ESTRUTURAS QUE SERÃO TRABALHADAS E DESENVOLVA AS HABILIDADES AUDITIVA E ORAL.

KEY WORDS

ESTE BOXE APRESENTA NOMES DE OBJETOS E DE PARTES DA CENA DE ABERTURA, QUE SERÃO ESTUDADOS AO LONGO DA LIÇÃO.

LANGUAGE TIME

ESTA SEÇÃO TRAZ ATIVIDADES QUE VÃO POSSIBILITAR QUE VOCÊ EXPLORE A LÍNGUA INGLESA DE FORMA SIMPLES E NATURAL.

NOW, WE KNOW!

MOMENTO DE VERIFICAR SE OS CONTEÚDOS FORAM COMPREENDIDOS POR MEIO DE ATIVIDADES DIVERSIFICADAS.

LET'S PRACTICE!

ESTA SEÇÃO PROPÕE ATIVIDADES PARA REFORÇAR O QUE FOI ESTUDADO NA LIÇÃO. VOCÊ VAI COLOCAR EM PRÁTICA O QUE APRENDEU NAS SEÇÕES ANTERIORES.

IT'S YOUR TURN!

ESTA SEÇÃO PROPÕE ATIVIDADES PROCEDIMENTAIS, EXPERIÊNCIAS OU VIVÊNCIAS PARA VOCÊ APRENDER NA PRÁTICA O CONTEÚDO ESTUDADO.

TALKING ABOUT...

A SEÇÃO TRAZ UMA SELEÇÃO DE TEMAS PARA REFLETIR, DISCUTIR E APRENDER MAIS, CAPACITANDO VOCÊ PARA ATUAR NO DIA A DIA COM MAIS CONSCIÊNCIA!

REVIEW

ESTA SEÇÃO TRAZ ATIVIDADES DE REVISÃO DE CADA UMA DAS LIÇÕES.

LET'S PLAY!

ATIVIDADES LÚDICAS PARA QUE VOCÊ APRENDA ENQUANTO SE DIVERTE!

MATERIAL COMPLEMENTAR

READER

LIVRO DE LEITURA QUE ACOMPANHA CADA VOLUME. A HISTÓRIA ESTIMULA A IMAGINAÇÃO E O CONHECIMENTO LINGUÍSTICO, À MEDIDA QUE LEVA VOCÊ A UMA AVENTURA EMOCIONANTE PELO MUNDO DA LITERATURA.

GLOSSARY

TRAZ AS PALAVRAS-CHAVE EM INGLÊS, ESTUDADAS AO LONGO DESTE VOLUME, SEGUIDAS DA TRADUÇÃO EM PORTUGUÊS.

QUANDO VOCÊ ENCONTRAR ESTES ÍCONES, FIQUE ATENTO!

- IN PAIRS
- IN GROUP
- SAY
- STICK
- WRITE
- DRAW
- CIRCLE
- MAKE AN X
- NUMBER
- COLOR
- DOT TO DOT
- MATCH
- LISTEN

CONTENTS

UNIT 1 — AT HOME 8

LESSON 1
FAMILY 10

LANGUAGE POINTS

FAMILY, MOM, DAD, BROTHER, SISTER, BABY BROTHER, DOG

HI, MY NAME IS... / HELLO! / THIS IS...

LESSON 2
HOUSE PARTS 18

LANGUAGE POINTS

BATHROOM, BEDROOM, KITCHEN, LIVING ROOM

WHERE IS...? / THIS IS...

TALKING ABOUT...: DIFFERENT FAMILY STRUCTURES 26

UNIT 2 — AT SCHOOL 28

LESSON 3
THE CLASSROOM 30

LANGUAGE POINTS

CLASSROOM, TEACHER, STUDENT, SCHOOLBAG, BOOK, PENCIL, ERASER, CRAYON

I AM...

LESSON 4
BREAK TIME 38

LANGUAGE POINTS

ONE, TWO, THREE, FOUR, FIVE, SIX, SEVEN, EIGHT, NINE, TEN

IT'S... / LET'S PLAY!

IT'S YOUR TURN!: DINOSAUR PENCIL HOLDER 46

UNIT 3 — ART AND SCIENCE 48

≋ LESSON 5 ≋
ART CLASS 50

LANGUAGE POINTS

ART, BLUE, BROWN, GREEN, ORANGE, PINK, RED, YELLOW

WHAT COLOR IS THIS?

≋ LESSON 6 ≋
SCIENCE CLASS 58

LANGUAGE POINTS

SCIENCE, ARM, FOOT, HAND, HEAD, LEG

LET'S LEARN...! / SHOW ME...

TALKING ABOUT...: SHOW ME YOUR HANDS! 66

UNIT 4 — THE CITY 68

≋ LESSON 7 ≋
THE PARK 70

LANGUAGE POINTS

PARK, TREE, FLOWER, CAT, BIRD, DOG, BALL, ICE CREAM

WHAT A LOVELY DAY!

≋ LESSON 8 ≋
THE SUPERMARKET 78

LANGUAGE POINTS

SUPERMARKET, APPLES, BANANAS, CHOCOLATE, COOKIES, EGGS, JUICE, MILK

DO YOU LIKE? / I LIKE...

IT'S YOUR TURN!: THE MINI MARKET 86

REVIEW 88
LET'S PLAY! 96
CELEBRATION SONGS 104
AUDIO TRANSCRIPT 105
GLOSSARY 106
SUGGESTIONS FOR STUDENTS 111
BIBLIOGRAPHY 112
MEMORY GAME 113
STICKERS

LESSON 1 — FAMILY

LISTEN AND SAY

KEY WORDS

1 LOOK, LISTEN AND SAY.

DAD — MOM

SISTER

LANGUAGE TIME

1 COLOR THE FAMILY AND SAY.

2 STICK AND SAY.

NOW, WE KNOW!

1 LISTEN AND MAKE AN **X**.

A)

B)

C)

 FOURTEEN

2 MATCH AND SAY.

HI, MY NAME IS PAT.

THIS IS MY FAMILY.

THIS IS MY BABY BROTHER.

LET'S PRACTICE!

1 DRAW A FAMILY MEMBER.

2 LOOK AND CIRCLE THE FAMILY MEMBERS.

DAD   MOM   BROTHER

3 LOOK AND MATCH.

LET'S SING!

HELLO, LILY!

HELLO!

HELLO, HELLO, HELLO!

WHAT IS YOUR NAME?

HELLO, HELLO, HELLO!

MY NAME IS LILY.

MY NAME IS LILY.

HELLO, LILY!

HELLO, LILY!

HELLO!

LESSON 2 — HOUSE PARTS

LISTEN AND SAY

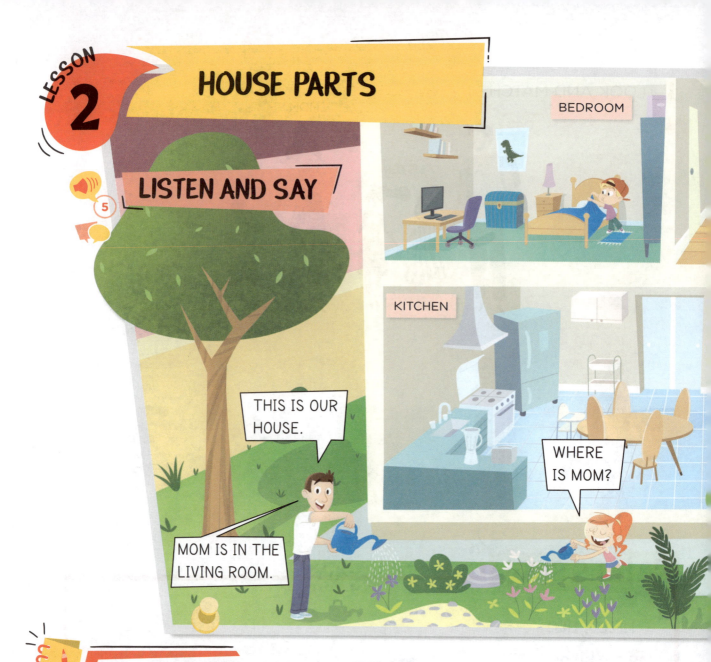

KEY WORDS

1 LOOK, LISTEN AND SAY.

LIVING ROOM

KITCHEN

1 POINT AND SAY.

LIVING ROOM

KITCHEN

BATHROOM

BEDROOM

2 COLOR AND SAY.

BATHROOM

BEDROOM

LIVING ROOM

NOW, WE KNOW!

1 MATCH AND SAY.

2 FIND THE WAY.

LET'S PRACTICE!

1 LISTEN AND NUMBER.

2 DRAW A FAMILY AT HOME.

🎵 LET'S SING!

I LOVE MY SWEET HOME!

I LOVE MY HOME
SWEET HOME, SWEET HOME!
I AM IN THE LIVING ROOM
TO SING AND PLAY
I AM IN THE KITCHEN
IT IS TIME TO EAT
I AM IN THE BATHROOM
TO TAKE A SHOWER
I AM IN MY BEDROOM!
IT IS TIME TO SLEEP!
YAWN!

TALKING ABOUT...

DIFFERENT FAMILY STRUCTURES

- WHAT DO THESE PHOTOS REPRESENT?
- WHAT IS NECESSARY TO BE A FAMILY?

1 DRAW YOUR FAMILY AND SHOW IT TO YOUR CLASSMATES.

2 WHAT IS SPECIAL ABOUT YOUR FAMILY? SHARE IT WITH YOUR CLASSMATES.

UNIT 2

AT SCHOOL

JOIN THE CIRCLE!
- WHAT DO YOU SEE IN THE PICTURE?
- WHO ARE THESE PEOPLE?
- WHERE ARE THEY GOING TO?

LET'S LEARN!
- SCHOOL OBJECTS
- NUMBERS 1 TO 10

LESSON 3

THE CLASSROOM

LISTEN AND SAY

KEY WORDS

1 LOOK, LISTEN AND SAY.

TEACHER   PENCIL   BOOK

ERASER　　CRAYON　　STUDENT　　SCHOOLBAG

1 STICK AND SAY.

2 MAKE AN X AND SAY.

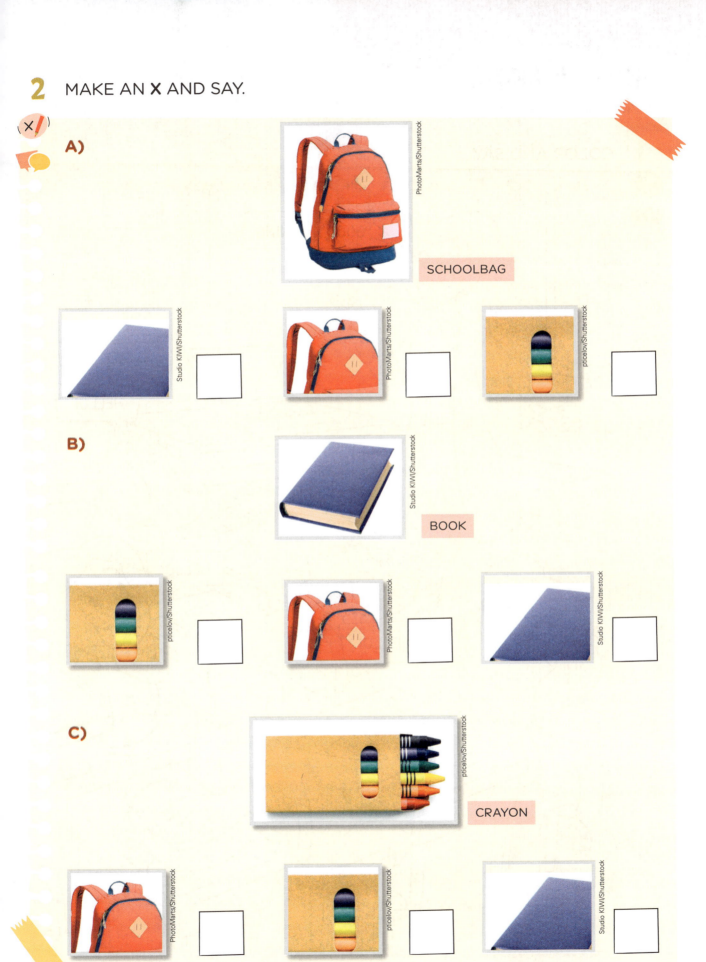

NOW, WE KNOW!

1 COLOR AND SAY.

2 CIRCLE THE SCHOOL OBJECTS.

2 CIRCLE THE SCHOOL OBJECTS FROM THE BOX AND SAY.

PENCIL	BOOK	ERASER	CRAYON	SCHOOLBAG

🎵 LET'S SING!

I AM SO VERY HAPPY

🔊 12

GOOD MORNING, DEAR FRIEND.
GOOD MORNING, HOW ARE YOU?
I AM SO VERY HAPPY,
TO SAY HELLO TO YOU.
GOOD AFTERNOON, DEAR FRIEND.
GOOD AFTERNOON, HOW ARE YOU?
I AM SO VERY HAPPY,
TO SAY HELLO TO YOU.

LESSON 4: BREAK TIME

LISTEN AND SAY

"IT'S BREAK TIME!"

KEY WORDS

1 LOOK, LISTEN AND SAY.

1 — ONE
2 — TWO
3 — THREE
4 — FOUR
5 — FIVE

SIX SEVEN EIGHT NINE TEN

1 COMPLETE AND SAY.

2 LISTEN AND CIRCLE.

A)

B)

C)

NOW, WE KNOW!

1 JOIN THE DOTS AND COLOR.

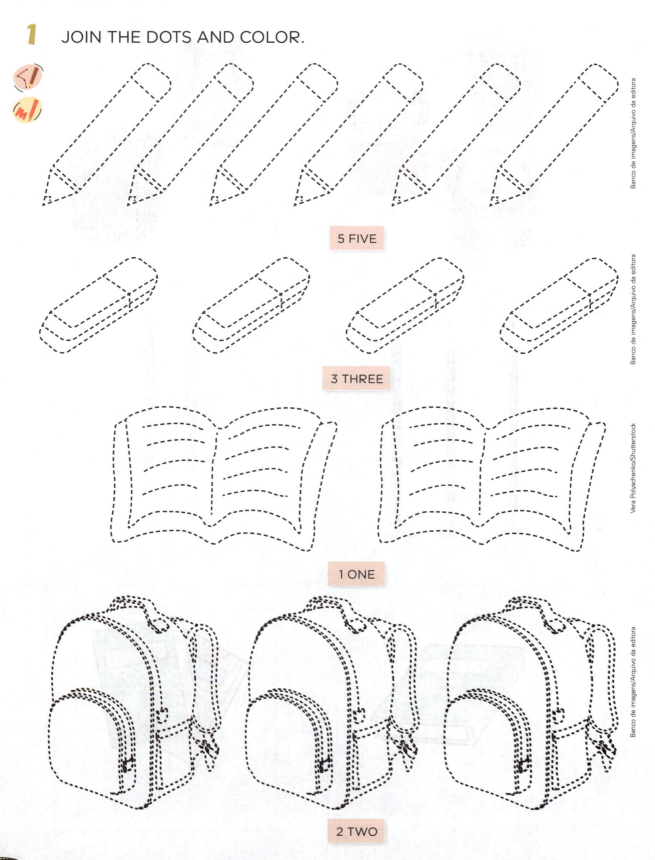

5 FIVE

3 THREE

1 ONE

2 TWO

2 COLOR AND SAY.

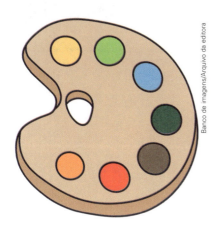

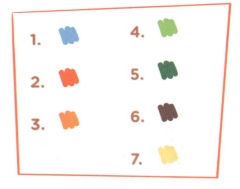

FORTY-THREE 43

LET'S PRACTICE!

1 FIND THE WAY TO SCHOOL.

2 LISTEN AND SAY.

LET'S SING!

10 BABY DINOSAURS

STEGOSAURUS!
1 BABY, 2 BABIES, 3 BABIES DINOSAUR,
4 BABIES, 5 BABIES, 6 BABIES DINOSAUR,
7 BABIES, 8 BABIES, 9 BABIES DINOSAUR,
10 LITTLE BABIES DINOSAUR.

TRICERATOPS!
1 BABY, 2 BABIES, 3 BABIES DINOSAUR,
4 BABIES, 5 BABIES, 6 BABIES DINOSAUR,
7 BABIES, 8 BABIES, 9 BABIES DINOSAUR,
10 LITTLE BABIES DINOSAUR.

PTERODACTYL!
1 BABY, 2 BABIES, 3 BABIES DINOSAURS,
4 BABIES, 5 BABIES, 6 BABIES DINOSAUR,
7 BABIES, 8 BABIES, 9 BABIES DINOSAUR,
10 LITTLE BABIES DINOSAUR
10 LITTLE BABIES DINOSAUR.

TECH TIPS...

YOU CAN WATCH CHILDREN´S CHANNELS AND ACCESS EDUCATIONAL SITES ON THE INTERNET TO LEARN AND SING OTHER CHILDREN´S SONGS AND NURSERY RHYMES IN ENGLISH.

IT'S YOUR TURN!

DINOSAUR PENCIL HOLDER

IN GROUPS, FOLLOW THE STEPS BELOW.

YOU NEED:

- 4 TOILET PAPER ROLLS

- DARK GREEN CREPE PAPER

- COLORED PENS AND PENCILS, CRAYONS, GLUE AND BLUNT-TIP SCISSORS

- COLORED CARDBOARD SHEETS (FOR THE BOTTOM OF THE ROLLS AND FOR THE DINOSAUR´S EYES)

1) PICK UP THE ROLLS AND GLUE THE BOTTOM.

2) COVER THE ROLLS WITH GREEN PAPER AND GLUE THEM.

3) DRAW, CUT AND GLUE THE DINOSAUR´S EYES. DRAW ITS MOUTH.

4) HERE IT IS! YOUR DINOSAUR PENCIL HOLDER.

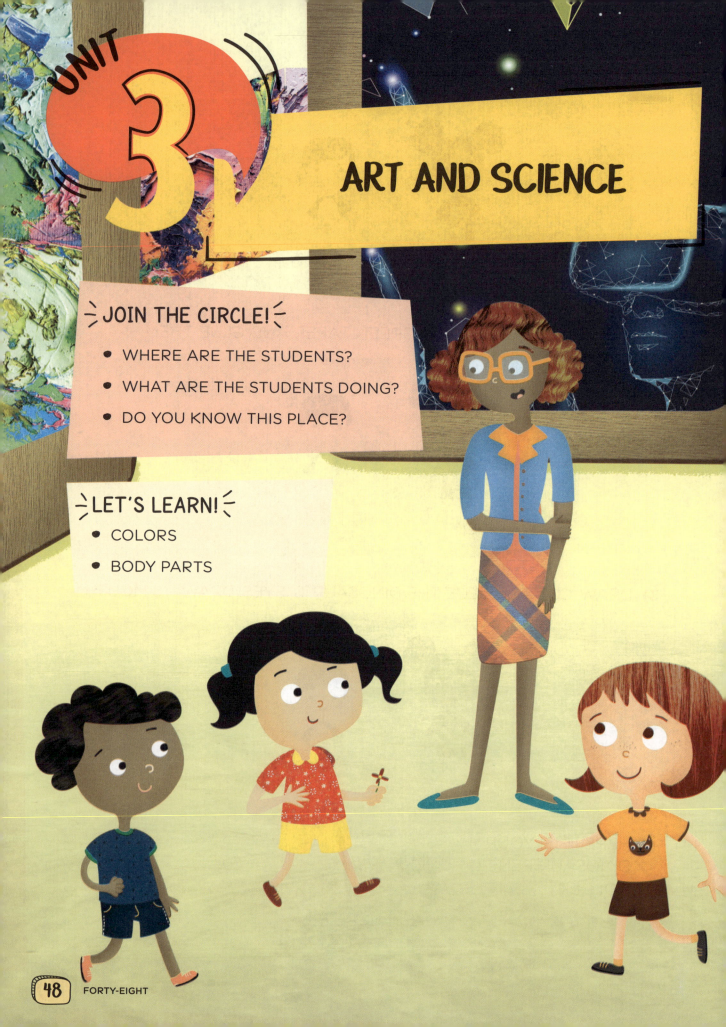

LESSON 5 — ART CLASS

LISTEN AND SAY

WHAT COLOR IS THIS?

KEY WORDS

1 LOOK, LISTEN AND SAY.

YELLOW

ORANGE

RED

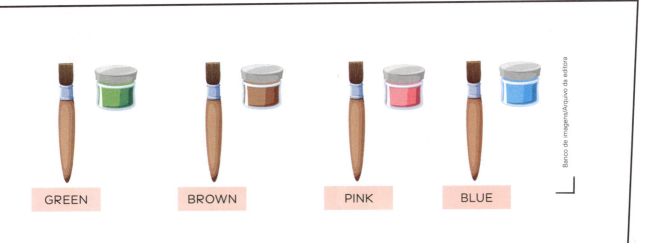

GREEN BROWN PINK BLUE

LANGUAGE TIME

1 STICK THE MISSING COLORS AND SAY.

2 LOOK AND NUMBER.

3

A)

Piet Mondrian/Collection Mr. and Mrs. Armand P. Bartos, New York, USA.

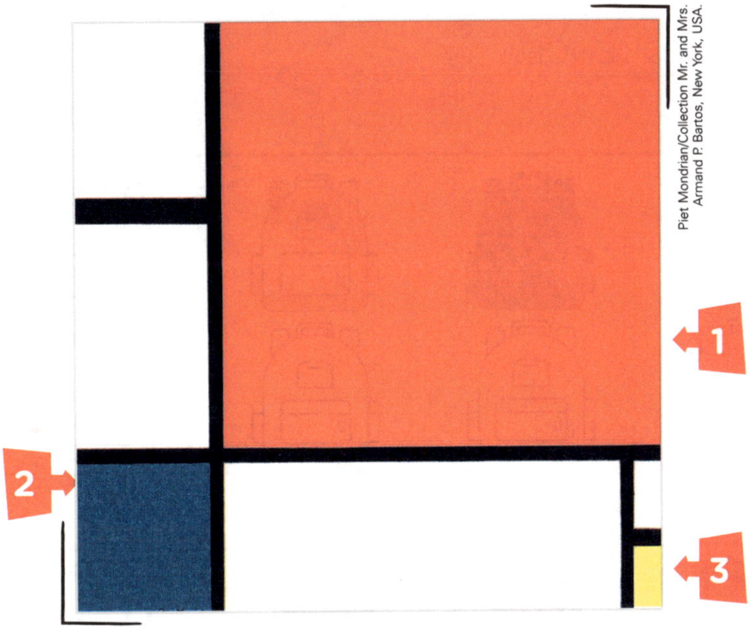

COMPOSITION WITH RED, BLUE AND YELLOW, PIET MONDRIAN, 1930.

☐ YELLOW ☐ RED ☐ BLUE

B)

De Agostini Picture Library/ Bridgeman/Fotoarena

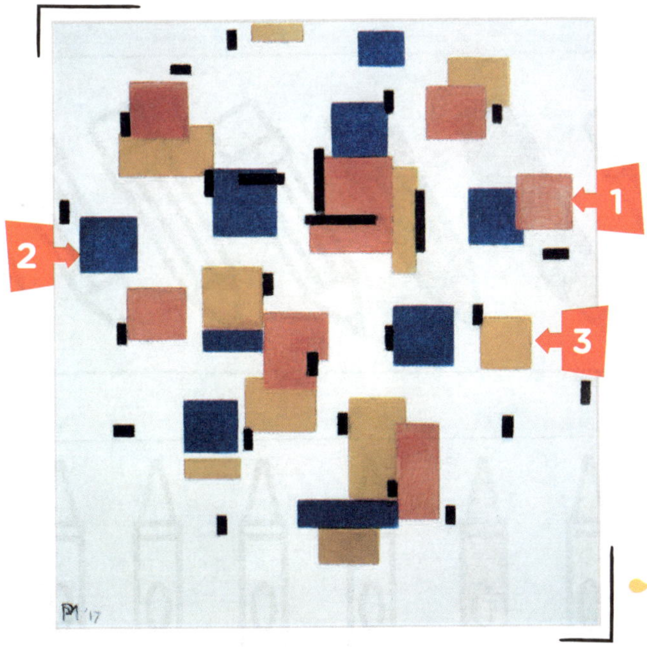

COMPOSITION IN COLOUR A, PIET MONDRIAN, 1917.

☐ BLUE ☐ ORANGE ☐ RED

NOW, WE KNOW!

1 COLOR THE SEQUENCE.

A)

B)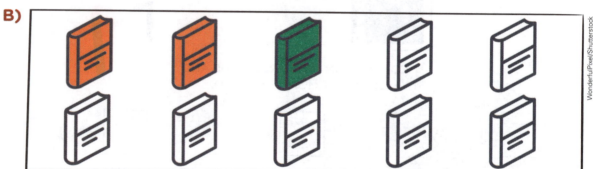

C)

D)

2 MATCH AND SAY.

BLUE  CRAYON

BROWN  SCHOOLBAG

GREEN  BOOK

PINK  PENCIL

LET'S PRACTICE!

1 LISTEN AND MAKE AN **X**.

20

A)

New Africa/Shutterstock

New Africa/Shutterstock

New Africa/Shutterstock

B)

Bogdan Florea/Shutterstock

pogonici/Shutterstock

CoolPhotoGirl/Shutterstock

C)

H_Ko/Shutterstock

alexvav/Shutterstock

bounward/Shutterstock

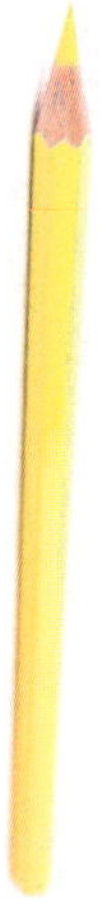

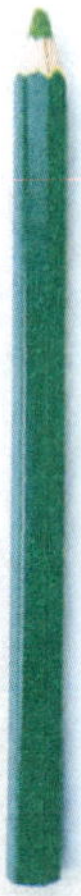

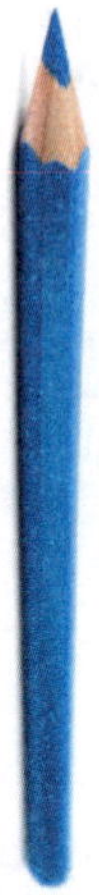

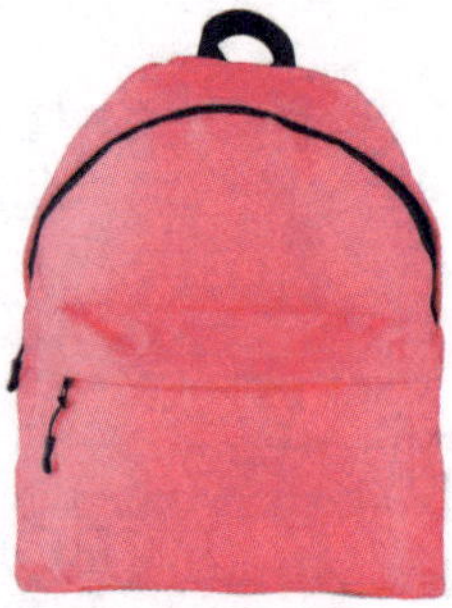

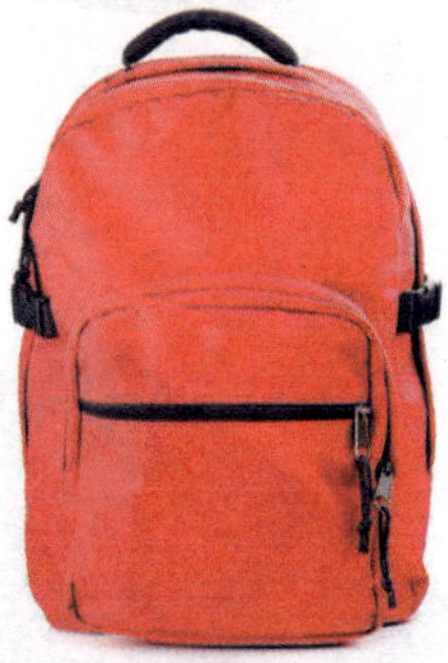

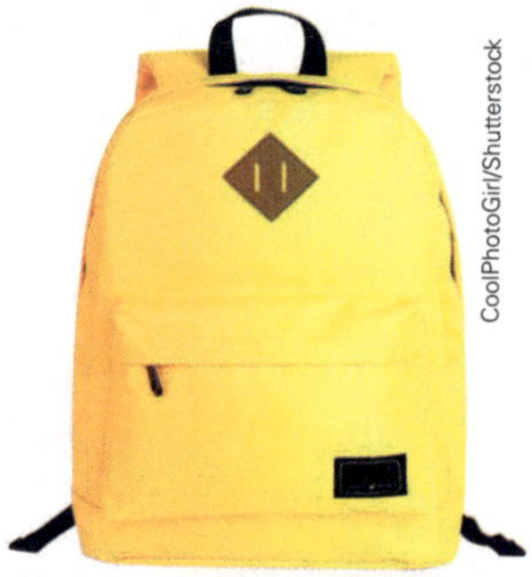

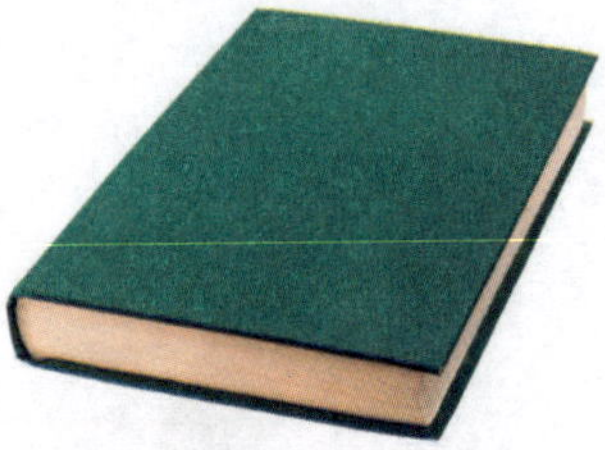

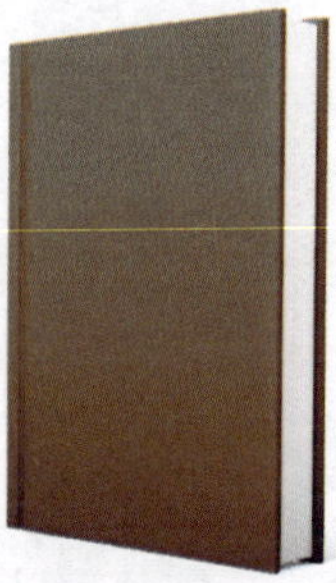

2 COLOR.

PINK ♣ BROWN ★ GREEN ● ORANGE ✿
BLUE ✸ YELLOW ◆ RED ✚

🎵 LET'S SING!

RAP OF THE COLORS

🔊 21

RED, YELLOW, PINK AND BLUE,

ORANGE, PURPLE, AND NAVY-BLUE,

I CAN SEE COLORS ALL AROUND ME,

COLORS FOR YOU, COLORS FOR ME!

SING IT AGAIN!

LESSON 6 — SCIENCE CLASS

LISTEN AND SAY

KEY WORDS

1 LOOK, LISTEN AND SAY.

 HEAD

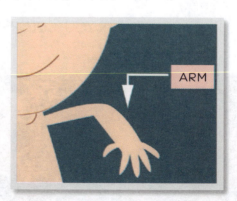 ARM

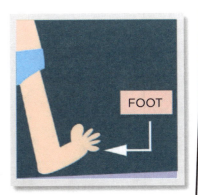

1 DRAW AND SAY.

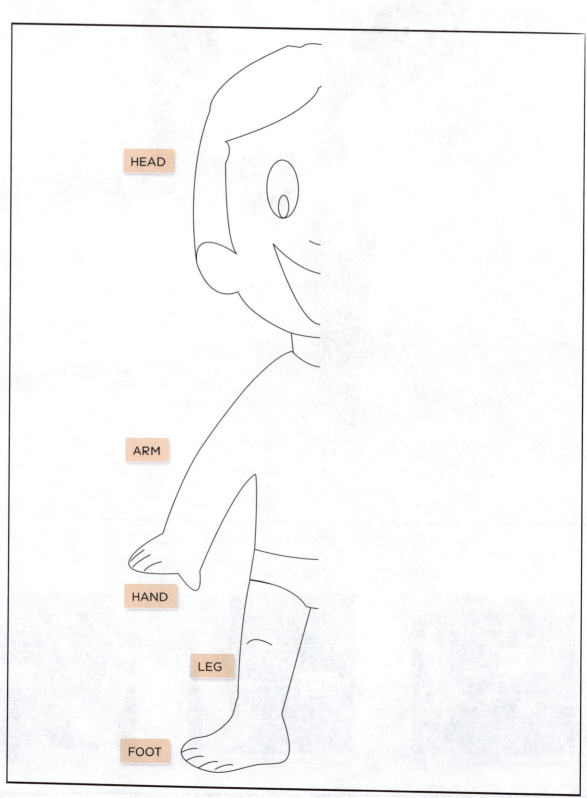

2 LISTEN AND CIRCLE.

NOW, WE KNOW!

1 COLOR AND SAY.

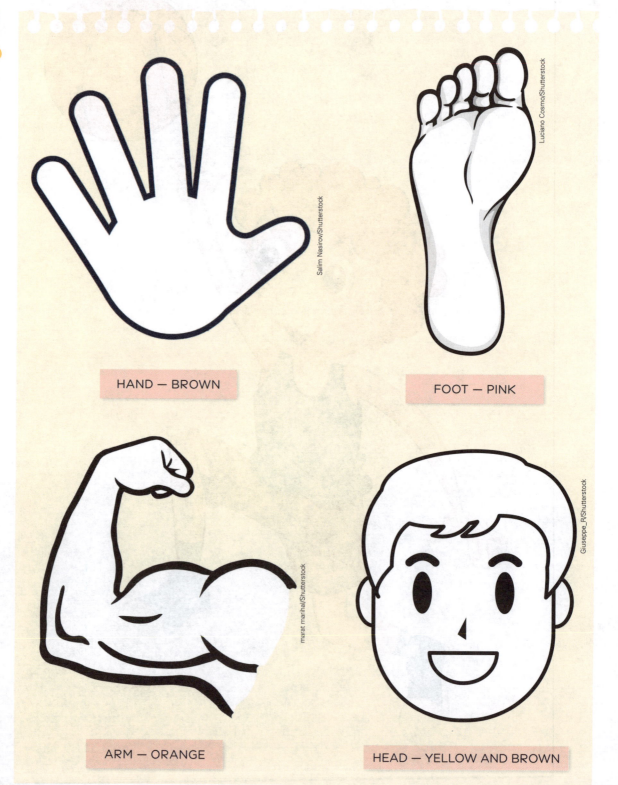

HAND — BROWN

FOOT — PINK

ARM — ORANGE

HEAD — YELLOW AND BROWN

2 MATCH.

ARM

HAND

HEAD

FOOT

LEG

LET'S PRACTICE!

1   FIND FIVE DIFFERENCES AND SAY.

LET'S SING!

THE HOKEY POKEY

YOU PUT YOUR RIGHT FOOT IN,
YOU TAKE YOUR RIGHT FOOT OUT,
YOU PUT YOUR RIGHT FOOT IN
AND YOU SHAKE IT ALL ABOUT.

YOU DO THE HOKEY POKEY
AND YOU TURN AROUND,
THAT'S WHAT IT'S ALL ABOUT.
OH! DO THE HOKEY POKEY (3X)
THAT'S WHAT IT'S ALL ABOUT.

YOU PUT YOUR LEFT FOOT IN,
YOU TAKE YOUR LEFT FOOT OUT,
YOU PUT YOUR LEFT FOOT IN,
AND YOU SHAKE IT ALL ABOUT.

YOU PUT YOUR RIGHT HAND IN,
YOU TAKE YOUR RIGHT HAND OUT,
YOU PUT YOUR RIGHT HAND IN,
AND YOU SHAKE IT ALL ABOUT.

YOU PUT YOUR LEFT HAND IN,
YOU TAKE YOUR LEFT HAND OUT,
YOU PUT YOUR LEFT HAND IN,
AND YOU SHAKE IT ALL ABOUT.

YOU PUT YOUR WHOLE SELF IN,
YOU TAKE YOUR WHOLE SELF OUT,
YOU PUT YOUR WHOLE SELF IN,
AND YOU SHAKE IT ALL ABOUT.

TALKING ABOUT...

SHOW ME YOUR HANDS!

- WHEN DO YOU WASH YOUR HANDS?
- WHY DO YOU WASH YOUR HANDS?
- HOW DO YOU WASH YOUR HANDS?

STEPS TO WASH YOUR HANDS PROPERLY

1. WET YOUR HANDS WITH CLEAN WATER.

2. APPLY SOAP.

3. SCRUB YOUR HANDS PALM TO PALM FOR 15 TO 20 SECONDS.

4. RUB BETWEEN YOUR FINGERS.

5. RINSE YOUR HANDS UNDER WATER.

6. DRY YOUR HANDS.

UNIT 4

THE CITY

JOIN THE CIRCLE!
- WHAT DO YOU SEE IN THE PICTURE?
- WHAT PLACES DO YOU KNOW?
- WHAT PLACES CAN YOU FIND IN YOUR CITY?

LET'S LEARN!
- PARK ELEMENTS
- FOOD

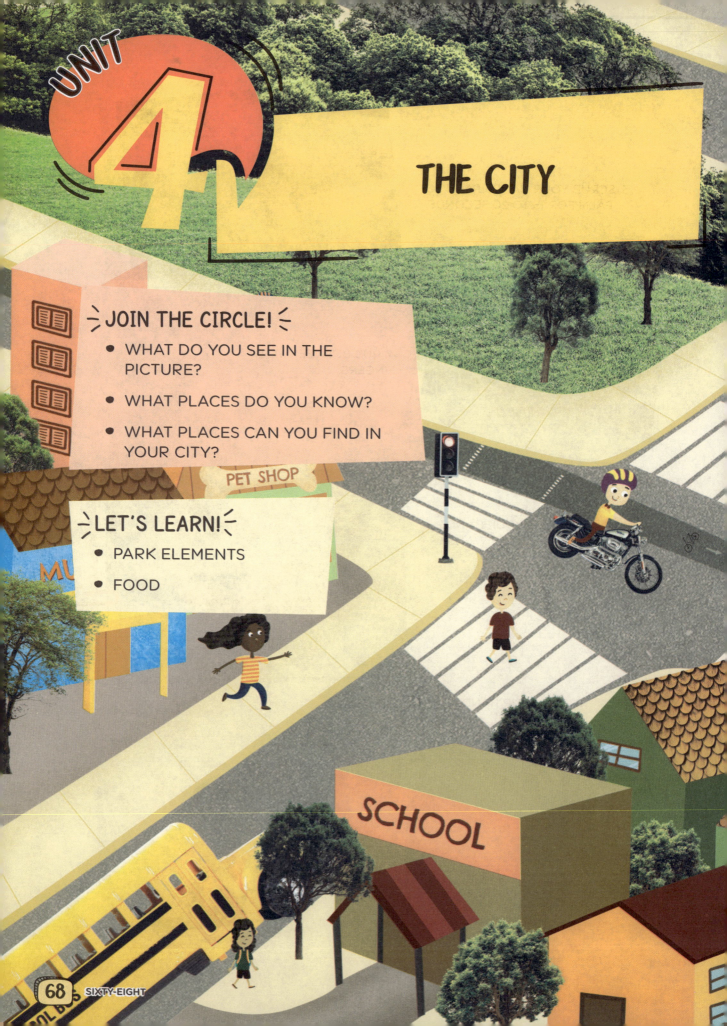

LESSON 7 — THE PARK

LISTEN AND SAY

WHAT A LOVELY DAY!

KEY WORDS

1 LOOK, LISTEN AND SAY.

BIRD

ICE CREAM

TREE

FLOWER BALL DOG CAT

LANGUAGE TIME

1 STICK AND SAY.

CAT

BIRD

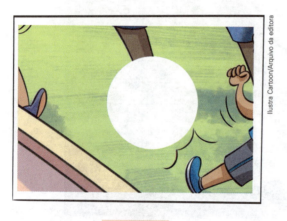
BALL

TREE

FLOWERS

DOG

2 COLOR AND SAY.

NOW, WE KNOW!

1 CIRCLE THE ODD ONE OUT AND SAY.

A) FLOWER

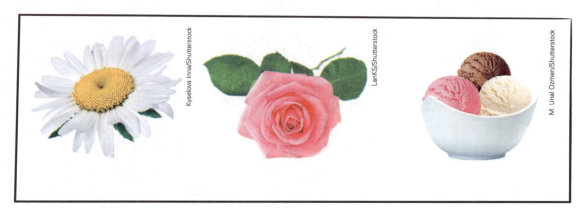

B) BIRD

C) TREE

2 LOOK AND MAKE AN X.

A) 
☐ ICE CREAM
☐ BALL

B) 
☐ DOG
☐ CAT

C) 
☐ HOUSE
☐ PARK

D) 
☐ TREE
☐ FLOWERS

SEVENTY-FIVE 75

LET'S PRACTICE!

1 LISTEN AND CIRCLE.

2 DRAW.

CAT	DOG	BIRD
FLOWER	TREE	BALL

 LET'S SING!

GOING TO THE PARK

(29) GOING TO THE PARK

LOVELY IDEA! EI, EI, OH

FLOWERS AND TREES

BIRDS AND BEES! EI, EI, OH

LOTS OF POPCORN

DELICIOUS ICE CREAM! EI, EI, OH

PLAY, PLAY HERE!

PLAY, PLAY THERE! EI, EI, OH

CLAP, CLAP

LESSON 8

THE SUPERMARKET

LISTEN AND SAY

30

KEY WORDS

1 LOOK, LISTEN AND SAY.

31

APPLES   COOKIES   MILK

78 SEVENTY-EIGHT

BANANAS

JUICE

EGGS

CHOCOLATE

1 STICK AND SAY.

2 LISTEN AND CIRCLE.

NOW, WE KNOW!

1 MATCH AND SAY.

2 DRAW THE SEQUENCE.

A)

B)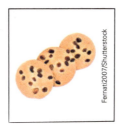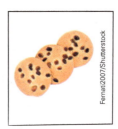

C)

EIGHTY-THREE **83**

LET'S PRACTICE!

1 FIND AND COLOR.

2 DRAW AND COLOR YOUR FAVORITE FRUIT.

🎵 LET'S SING!

AT THE SUPERMARKET

TAKE AN APPLE JUICE
A CARTON OF MILK
AND PUT THEM IN THE
SHOPPING CART.

SING THIS CHANT
AND TURN AROUND
THAT IS WHAT I SAY. (3X)

GOOD TIME AT THE SUPERMARKET
BUT WHAT A LONG SHOPPING LIST!

TAKE AN ORANGE JUICE,
A BUNCH OF BANANAS
AND PUT THEM IN THE
SHOPPING CART.

SING THIS CHANT
AND TURN AROUND
THAT IS WHAT I SAY. (3X)

GOOD TIME AT THE SUPERMARKET
BUT WHAT A LONG SHOPPING LIST!

IT'S YOUR TURN!

THE MINI MARKET

IN GROUPS, FOLLOW THE STEPS BELOW.

YOU NEED:

- EMPTY CARTONS OF MILK AND JUICE

- COOKIES AND CHOCOLATE EMPTY PACKAGES

- PACKAGES OF EGGS, APPLES AND BANANAS

- COLORED PENCILS AND PENS, CRAYONS, GLUE AND PAPERS

1) PICK THE PRODUCTS AND ORGANIZE THEM ON DESKS AND CHAIRS AROUND THE CLASSROOM.

2) WRITE THE NAME OF EACH PRODUCT ON A TAG.

3) NOW, IT'S TIME TO ACT. WRITE DOWN A SHOPPING LIST ON A PIECE OF PAPER.

4) THEN, GO TO THE CLASSROOM MINI MARKET AND BUY ALL THE PRODUCTS YOU HAVE ON YOUR SHOPPING LIST.

REVIEW — FAMILY

1 CIRCLE THE MOM.

A)

B)

C)

D)

2 DRAW YOUR FAMILY OR GLUE A PHOTO.

REVIEW  HOUSE PARTS

1 LOOK AND MAKE AN **X**.

A) LIVING ROOM

B) BATHROOM

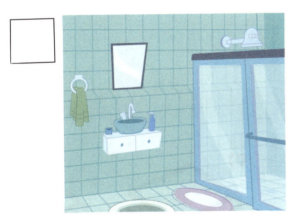 

2 DRAW YOUR BEDROOM.

EIGHTY-NINE 89

REVIEW  THE CLASSROOM

1 COLOR THE SCHOOL OBJECTS.

1. RED 2. YELLOW 3. BLUE 4. GREEN 5. PINK 6. ORANGE

A)

B)
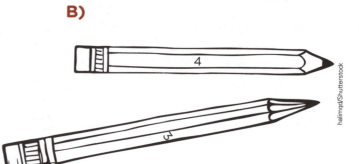

C)

D)
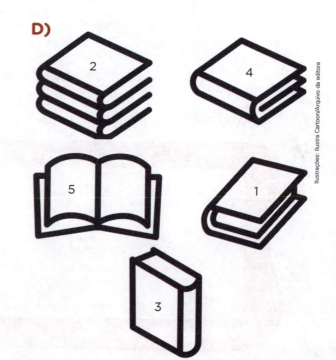

REVIEW — BREAK TIME

1 NUMBER AND SAY.

A)

B)

C)

REVIEW — ART CLASS

1 COLOR THE PICTURE.

1	2	3	4	5	6	7
GREEN	YELLOW	ORANGE	BLUE	BROWN	RED	PINK

REVIEW  SCIENCE CLASS

1 LOOK AND NUMBER THE BODY PARTS.

1. LEG   2. ARM   3. HAND   4. HEAD   5. FOOT

REVIEW → THE PARK

1 COUNT AND MATCH.

TWO CATS

THREE BIRDS

FOUR FLOWERS

ONE TREE

REVIEW  THE SUPERMARKET

1 DRAW A FOOD MARKET.

| MILK | CHOCOLATE | APPLES | BANANAS | EGGS | COOKIES |

- DRAW YOUR FAVORITE FOOD.

LET'S PLAY! → FAMILY

1 CIRCLE THE IDENTICAL PICTURES.

2 DRAW AND COLOR A BIG FAMILY.

LET'S PLAY! **HOUSE PARTS**

1 FIND THREE DIFFERENCES, CIRCLE AND SAY.

LET'S PLAY! → **THE CLASSROOM**

1 FIND THE WAY TO THE SCHOOL OBJECTS.

LET'S PLAY! ⇒ BREAK TIME

1 COLOR AND SAY.

1 ✤
2 ✤
3 ✤
4 ✤
5 ✤
6 ✤
7 ✤

2 COMPLETE WITH THE NUMBERS.

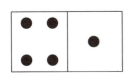   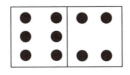   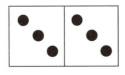

.... + ... = ... + ... = ... + ... = ...

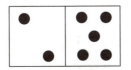   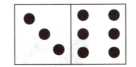   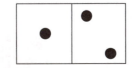

.... + ... = ... + ... = ... + ... = ...

NINETY-NINE **99**

LET'S PLAY! → ART CLASS

1 MAKE AN **X** ON THE COLORS IN THE PAINTING.

- *WOMAN TORSO*, KAZIMIR MALEVICH, 1932.

☐ YELLOW
☐ BLUE
☐ BROWN
☐ ORANGE
☐ PINK

2 CIRCLE YOUR FAVORITE COLOR.

MY FAVORITE COLOR IS...

LET'S PLAY! SCIENCE CLASS

1 WORD SEARCH.

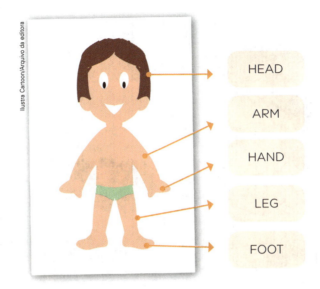

H	A	N	D	F	I
X	A	T	M	W	R
A	E	F	O	O	T
D	C	G	C	T	F
J	R	L	E	X	D
R	M	I	L	E	G
A	R	M	A	T	X
A	H	H	E	A	D

ONE HUNDRED AND ONE 101

LET'S PLAY! THE PARK

1 FIND FIVE DIFFERENCES, CIRCLE AND SAY.

LET'S PLAY! → THE SUPERMARKET

1 COLOR THE HEALTHY FOODS.

- PIZZA

- APPLE

- ORANGE JUICE

- HOT DOG

- BANANA

- HAMBURGER

- MILK

- ORANGE

- PAPAYA

CELEBRATION SONGS

VALENTINE'S CHANT

YOU'RE MY FRIEND
MY BEST FRIEND
YOU'RE MY VALENTINE
YOU'RE MY VALENTINE

EASTER BUNNY

EASTER BUNNY,

EASTER BUNNY,

WHAT DO YOU BRING TO ME?

ONE EGG, TWO EGGS, THREE EGGS, SO, SO!

ONE EGG, TWO EGGS, THREE EGGS, SO, SO!

FAMILY DAY

OH! HAPPY DAY

OH! HAPPY DAY

IT'S FAMILY DAY

IT'S FAMILY DAY

WE ARE ALL TOGETHER

WE ARE ALL TOGETHER

SINGING WHAT A HAPPY DAY!

LOVE FAMILY!

WHAT A HAPPY DAY!

LOVE FAMILY!

WHAT A HAPPY DAY!

GIVING THANKS

IF YOU'RE THANKFUL AND YOU KNOW IT SAY HURRAY!
HURRAY!
IF YOU'RE THANKFUL AND YOU KNOW IT SAY HURRAY!
HURRAY!
IF YOU'RE THANKFUL AND YOU KNOW IT AND YOUR SMILE REALLY SHOWS IT.
IF YOU'RE THANKFUL AND YOU KNOW IT SAY HURRAY!
HURRAY!

WE WISH YOU A MERRY CHRISTMAS

WE WISH YOU A MERRY CHRISTMAS,
WE WISH YOU A MERRY CHRISTMAS,
WE WISH YOU A MERRY CHRISTMAS
AND A HAPPY NEW YEAR.

AUDIO TRANSCRIPT

TRACK 3
A) BROTHER; B) MOM; C) DAD.

TRACK 7
1) KITCHEN; 2) LIVING ROOM;
3) BATHROOM; 4) BEDROOM.

TRACK 11
A) STUDENT; B) TEACHER; C) BOOK;
D) PENCIL; E) SCHOOLBAG;
F) CRAYON.

TRACK 15
A) THREE SCHOOLBAGS; B) TWO PENCILS; C) ONE BOOK.

TRACK 20
A) A YELLOW PENCIL; B) A RED SCHOOLBAG; C) A BROWN BOOK.

TRACK 24
HEAD; ARM; FOOT.

TRACK 28
ICE CREAM; DOG; BALL; TREE.

TRACK 32
APPLE; JUICE; EGGS; COOKIES.

GLOSSARY

BODY PARTS

ARM

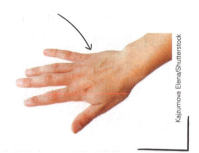
HAND

FOOT

HEAD

LEG

COLORS

 BLUE

 BROWN

 ORANGE

 GREEN

 PINK

 RED

 YELLOW

FAMILY MEMBERS

MOM/MOTHER

DAD/FATHER

SISTER

BROTHER

BABY BROTHER

GLOSSARY

● FOOD

APPLE

BANANA

CHOCOLATE

COOKIES

ICE CREAM

JUICE

EGG

MILK

● HOUSE PARTS

BATHROOM

BEDROOM

KITCHEN

LIVING ROOM

GLOSSARY

● NATURE

BIRD   CAT   DOG

FLOWER   TREE

● NUMBERS

ONE   TWO

THREE   FOUR

GLOSSARY

FIVE

SIX

SEVEN

EIGHT

NINE

TEN

PLACES

HOUSE

PARK

SCHOOL

GLOSSARY

SCHOOL

BOOK

CLASSROOM

CRAYON

ERASER

SCHOOLBAG

STUDENT

TEACHER

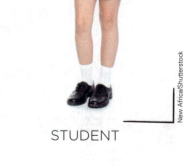
PENCIL

TOYS

BALL

DOLL

110 ONE HUNDRED AND TEN

SUGGESTIONS FOR STUDENTS

BOOKS

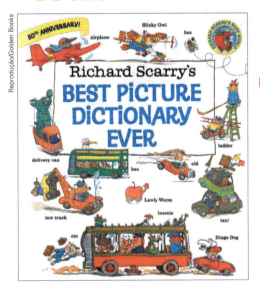

▶ RICHARD SCARRY. **RICHARD SCARRY'S BEST PICTURE DICTIONARY EVER**. NEW YORK: GOLDEN BOOKS, 2016.

LIVRO COM CERCA DE 2500 PALAVRAS E QUE APRESENTA 1000 IMAGENS, FAZENDO COM QUE OS ALUNOS APRENDAM POR MEIO DE DESCOBERTAS E BRINCADEIRAS.

▶ ERIC CARLE. **1, 2, 3 TO THE ZOO: A COUNTING BOOK**. NEW YORK: WORLD OF ERIC CARLE, 2019.

ESSE LIVRO, QUE MOSTRA ANIMAIS INDO PARA O ZOOLÓGICO DE TREM, EXPLORA NÚMEROS, CONTAGEM E SOMAS.

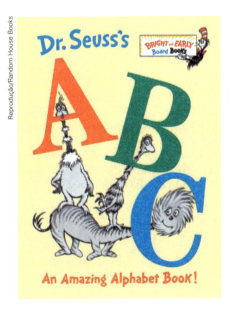

▶ DR. SEUSS. **DR. SEUSS'S ABC: AN AMAZING ALPHABET BOOK!** TORONTO: RANDOM HOUSE BOOKS FOR YOUNG READERS, 2014.

ESTE LIVRO DO DR. SEUSS, QUE VAI DE *AUNT ANNIE'S ALLIGATOR* ATÉ *ZIZZER-ZAZZER-ZUZZ*, É UM GUIA PARA A APRENDIZAGEM DO ALFABETO EM INGLÊS DE MANEIRA DIVERTIDA!

SITES

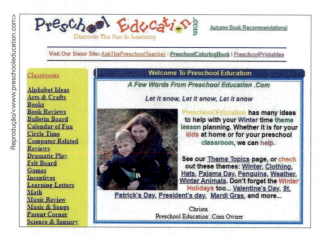

▶ www.preschooleducation.com

ATIVIDADES DE COLORIR, CANÇÕES E POEMAS ORGANIZADOS POR TEMAS.

▶ www.mamalisa.com

CANÇÕES, RECEITAS, POEMAS, ARTES E ARTESANATOS DO MUNDO.

▶ www.primarygames.com

JOGOS ON-LINE, HISTÓRIAS, ARTES, ATIVIDADES DE COLORIR, QUEBRA-CABEÇAS E MUITO MAIS.

BIBLIOGRAPHY

ALMEIDA FILHO, J. C. P. *DIMENSÕES COMUNICATIVAS NO ENSINO DE LÍNGUAS*. 2. ED. CAMPINAS: PONTES, 2000.

BRASIL. *BASE NACIONAL COMUM CURRICULAR (BNCC)*. BRASÍLIA: MEC, 2018. DISPONÍVEL EM: <http://basenacionalcomum.mec.gov.br/>. ACESSO EM: 26 SET. 2019.

CELANI, M. A. A. *ENSINO DE SEGUNDA LÍNGUA*: REDESCOBRINDO AS ORIGENS. SÃO PAULO: EDUC, 1997.

HARMER, J. *THE PRACTICE OF ENGLISH LANGUAGE TEACHING*. 4. ED. LONDON: PEARSON LONGMAN, 2007.

MOITA LOPES, L. P. A NOVA ORDEM MUNDIAL, OS PARÂMETROS CURRICULARES NACIONAIS E O ENSINO DE INGLÊS NO BRASIL. A BASE INTELECTUAL PARA UMA AÇÃO POLÍTICA. IN: BARBARA, L.; RAMOS, R. DE C. G. *REFLEXÃO E AÇÕES NO ENSINO-APRENDIZAGEM DE LÍNGUAS*. SÃO PAULO: MERCADO DE LETRAS, 2003.

VYGOTSKY, L. S. *A FORMAÇÃO SOCIAL DA MENTE*: O DESENVOLVIMENTO DOS PROCESSOS PSICOLÓGICOS SUPERIORES. SÃO PAULO: MARTINS FONTES, 1991.

MEMORY GAME

| DAD | MOM | FOOT | HAND |

| BEDROOM | ICE CREAM | JUICE | APPLE |

| BIRD | KITCHEN |

ommus/Shutterstock

djoyo art/Shutterstock

Ahmed zaki/Shutterstock

Ham_dee/Shutterstock

MicroOne/Shutterstock

Quarta/Shutterstock

Wth/Shutterstock

Vectors Bang/Shutterstock

Chereliss/Shutterstock

Adi Heriyanto/Shutterstock

ONE HUNDRED AND SEVENTEEN 117

| FLOWER | TREE | DOG | CAT |

| SCHOOLBAG | BOOK | SCHOOL | PARK |

| BALL | CRAYON |

STICKERS

🔴 LESSON 1 FAMILY

🔴 LESSON 3 THE CLASSROOM

🔴 LESSON 5 ART CLASS

LESSON 7 THE PARK

LESSON 8 THE SUPERMARKET

SIMON SAYS...

ELIETE CANESI MORINO
RITA BRUGIN DE FARIA

ALUNO: ....
ESCOLA: .... TURMA: ....

editora scipione